JANE.
HOPE GETS
BACK UP,
EVERY TIME.

♡, ANACHRISTINA

To Chris, Nick, and Colin.

Through you I've learned and grown more than I could ever ask or imagine.

You are my best.

I love you,

Mom.

Para mi Mamane, Julieta, quien era una mujer increíble.

Te quiero.

To my grandmother, who was an incredible woman.

I love you.

1908-2010

Ten percent of my printed books have been
given freely to those who
"need it the most today."

Pay it forward.

Photo Credits:

Bird of Paradise cover photo, canva.com

Lago de Atitlan, Guatemala, pg. 40: Ana-Christina

Author photos:: Barbara Peck

Blueprint, pg. 74, canva.com

TOOLS OF
HOPE

RESTORE AND RENEW YOUR HOPE

ANA-CHRISTINA HICKS
Career Resilience Coach | Speaker
www.toolsofhope.com

There is no despair so absolute as that which comes with the first moments of our first great sorrow, when we have not yet known what it is to have suffered and be healed, to have despaired and have recovered hope.

Mary Ann Evans—
Pen name George Eliot
(1819-1880)

Foreword:

 *1996*

I am pinned to the wall by my throat and my feet are barely touching the floor. He's in my face speaking in low threatening tones and the loathing spills out of his eyes. I'm being choked and I can't scream. Even if I could, I wouldn't because the boys will hear me. I can't live like this anymore. If this is life, I don't know if I want to live.

I used to take walks often in order to escape the hopeless situation in which I'd found myself. As I walked along the frozen beach, the brutal wind raged and the frigid salt air stung my face. In the darkness, the waves crashed onto the volcanic sand and I was thankful to be away from the abuse and chaos that had become my home.

At the time, I was living on a tiny Alaskan island which is the tip of an extinct volcano popping out of the Bering Sea.

I got married in my early twenties and moved to Wyoming after going to school in Colorado. I had two toddler boys and was pregnant with my third when we moved to St. Paul Island, Alaska. My marriage was already in trouble at that time, and got worse over the next four years.

Have you ever heard about those frog experiments? How, if you put a frog in a pot of hot, hot water, it'll jump out and save itself? BUT, if you put it in warm water and slowly heat the pot, **it will boil to death.**

I know, it's sick, but true. It's also a good analogy for a lot of domestic violence situations. It doesn't start out ugly. It typically grows ugly over time. And by that time, the victim has an investment in the relationship. Emotion. Connection. Children. Time. It's strange, because none of us really wants to acknowledge that it's happening, but the fact is that one out of every two women you know has been, or is being, abused physically, psychologically, or sexually. Domestic violence knows no boundaries. Rich or poor, any race, any neighborhood, any age, any level of education or socioeconomic group. The dynamics are well documented. (See Resources on page 106.)

Back to the story…

I'm isolated on an island, and growing more hopeless over time. I am confused because I don't really know how to move forward. I want to stay married because I made a promise. But don't want to be married and raise my boys with a role model of abuse and violence.

Because I never know when he's going to blow up, I'm always on pins and needles. When it does happen, I am shoved, hit, beaten, head butted until my entire face bruises down to my jaw. I have various items thrown at me, am thrown around, strangled, pinned to the ground, and restrained forcibly. The worst, though, is the criticism and belittling. My spirit is beaten down. I feel dumb, useless, and hopeless and have absolutely no energy left.

After he blows up, he comes back and says he's so sorry and that he'll never do it again.

But he always does.

The cycle of violence was full-blown in our little house on the tundra.

It was at this point that God, I am certain, sent a guardian angel to help me see more clearly. A woman to whom I'll forever be grateful for helping me see that there were other choices. She taught me about boundaries. She gave me strength when I felt like I was so weak. She showed me that my situation was more desperate and dangerous than I'd thought. (Remember the frog in the water that was heating up? That was me.)

She helped me put together an escape plan. That was Thursday. I ended up escaping on Saturday's flight. I was worried about getting caught by him and having him hurt me or one of my boys. Our only way off the island was by plane. And the three flights per week were often delayed or cancelled due to bad weather. I hadn't slept since Wednesday night, hadn't eaten, and I was sick with anxiety. My body was in full "fight or flight" mode. The boys and I caught the plane and after several transfers, landed in Denver the next day on a beautiful sunny Sunday afternoon with no luggage, a box, and a backpack.

I marked that Sunday as the birthday of starting a new life.

Since then, I have gotten and given education on domestic violence, I've changed careers, and I had the honor and pleasure of speaking and providing resiliency training for thousands of helping professionals.

What were you built for? Helping others see more clearly who they are, make different choices in their lives regarding their communication skills, their relationships, their finances, their values, and setting their priorities and taking accountability in their lives is my passion. It fills my heart to know that I make a difference.

Soooo...

You can set different rules for your kids, but if your parenting model doesn't change, the trouble remains.

With or without a partner, life can still be crazy.

You can move three thousand miles away and it won't fix anything if your heart hasn't changed.

You can change your job, but your attitude won't change unless your heart is different.

A marriage or divorce doesn't necessarily "fix" anything.

A surgery or remission doesn't necessarily "repair" everything.

In short... if you keep following the same patterns, the results will end up just the same. You can run, but if you don't heal the wound, you end up in the same tough place.

You can make all the outward changes in the world, but <u>if your heart doesn't change</u>, **the pain remains.**

AND... there IS something that can create change...

> The future is not a result of choices among alternative paths offered by the present, but a place that is created — created first in the mind and the will, created next in activity. The future is not some place we are going to, but one we are creating. The paths are not to be found, but made, and the activity of making them, changes both the maker and the destination.
>
> John Schaar, Futurist

Seeking tools to restore your **HOPE**.

Rebuilding habits.

Rebuilding yourself.

It seems daunting,

and

THE REWARDS ARE BEYOND BELIEF.

HOPE

HOPE

When life is tough, you need a different way to look at the situation.

A different tool.

Tools of Hope gives you simple tools to help you re-focus and bring **HOPE** back into your life.

To help you look up

and into H O P E.

When the world says
"Give up,"

Hope whispers
"Try it one more time."

Author Unknown

Pain in life is difficult
and can be overwhelming.

Circumstances can leave you upset, sad,
and hopeless.

It could be one **HUGE** thing.

Or a bunch of tiny little things that get heavy
and *weigh* *you* **down.**

So far down that you don't know how
or don't have the strength
to take the next step.

Sometimes grief threatens
to swamp you.

Sometimes, you just feel like you
"should" be content. But aren't.
"Should" have energy.

But don't.

Hopelessness
takes away

your clear thinking

your chances

your choices

your peace

your heart

your faith

your will

your love

your...

self

Have you ever tried to pound a nail without a hammer?

Oh, you try to find something hard enough, and heavy enough to set the nail, but it usually doesn't end up well. The fake "hammer" you found (a shoe, a wrench, a rock) usually either can't do the job or it ends up making a mess on the wall and on the floor (and probably on your thumb, too). You give it a good try, but often you end up wasting time and energy and go in search of the real hammer that you should have used in the first place.

Wrenches are good, and so are pliers, but if you need to drive a nail... a hammer is the best tool.

Any job usually takes longer and is frustrating <u>without the right tools</u>.

Would it be
worth it to
LEARN
about some
real, simple
tools that
would increase
your hope?

When you're down, it will help to **GAIN PERSPECTIVE** so you can make better choices, won't it?

Would it be
valuable to
BE
REMINDED
of some
techniques
you can use to
restore balance
into your life?

HOPE

gives you
the gift of

another chance

clear thinking

an open heart

your will

choice

peace

faith

love

your...

SELF

The three essentials to happiness in
this life are something to do,
something to love,
and something to hope for.

Joseph Addison (1672-1719)

ONCE YOU
CHOOSE
HOPE,
ANYTHING'S
POSSIBLE.

Christopher Reeve
(1952-2004)

HOPE
LOOKS
AND
SEES

WITH
AN
ETERNALLY
YOUNG
HEART.

Nothing is so strong as gentleness,

nothing so gentle as real strength.

Saint Francis de Sales (1567-1622)

A strong mind always hopes, and has always cause to hope.

- Thomas Carlyle (1795-1891)

HOPE
IS
STRONG

Victory and defeat are doors.

We only welcome these guests as much as we turn the knob.

Chris M. Hoffman, age 14

Most of the important things in the world have been accomplished by people who have kept on trying when there seemed to be no hope at all.

- Dale Carnegie (1898-1955)

HOPE GETS BACK UP.

EVERY TIME.

Do not be afraid.

Stand firm and you will see what the Lord your God will do to save you today...He will fight for you and all you have to do is keep still.

Exodus 14:13-14 (NIV)

HOPE
STANDS...

Hope is faith holding its hand
out in the dark.

George Iles

In order for the light to shine so
brightly, the darkness must be
present.

Francis Bacon (1561-1626)

HOPE
STANDS
patiently.

HOPE IS PATIENT.
HOPE STANDS FIRM.
HOPE WAITS FOR THE
SUNRISE.

Hope is the
thing with
feathers
that
perches in
the soul.

And sings
the tunes
without the
words,

and never
stops at all.

Emily
Dickenson
(1830-1886)

HOPE

SMILES

AND

LAUGHS

IN THE FACE OF FEAR,
UNCERTAINTY, DOUBT,
AND CONFUSION.

HOPE

HAS MANY FACES...

HOPE

STANDS
STILL.

HOPE

MOVES
FORWARD.

HOPE

EMBRACES CHANGE.

HOPE

SIGHS in the darkness...

as it remembers the light, the warmth of the sun, the strong scent of a blooming rose, the fresh smell of newly cut grass, the comfort of love…

And then
it stands tall
to take the
<u>first step forward</u>
to recapture
what it
remembers.

TOOLS OF HOPE

#1: **BREATHE**

Your body can't help but respond.

Breathing calms you down and allows your brain to think and be more logical instead of feeling out of control.

By breathing slowly and deeply, YOU make the choice to combat the "fight or flight" response that gets the best of you when you are worried, scared, upset, nervous or angry.

Make the **CHOICE**.
Consciously slow yourself down.

Be mindful of each cool, crisp breath you draw and exhale, without effort. Fill your lungs to capacity, and exhale as slowly as you can.

Take ten **deep, sloooow** breaths. If you start thinking about what is upsetting you— start over!

You're taking this all in!

You can do this anywhere - business meeting, awkward situation, upsetting confrontation, when you're bummed out and feeling unhappy...

#2:
Take care of yourself

Exercise your body.

Ya I know you know!
But are you DOING it?

Exercise your mind.

What are you trying that is new?

Exercise your soul.

What are you doing to discover your gifts, enrich your soul, light up your passions?

And if one day is too much—try one hour, or even one minute at a time. Hang in there!!

Get a massage manicure, or pedicure. Enjoy.

Take a bath!

A soak in a warm tub can ease a busy mind and relax your body.

Can't easily get away from the children? Plan a fun outing or activity for the whole family and **ENJOY THE MOMENT.**

A stroller walk, a trip to the zoo, a frosted batch of cookies (eat as you go!), a giggle with your little ones.

If you are depressed and sleeping too much, reach out to at least two trusted friends or family members and let them know what is going on. If it continues, consult your doctor or therapist.

How about the little (BIG) things?

Are you **sleeping** enough, **drinking** enough water, and **eating** right?

Do something that relaxes you.

I know, you say you don't have enough time...but make the time to do what's important for you.

Take the time to prepare and cook healthy, delicious (hey—it's possible!) food for yourself.

Tell your secrets to someone furry. Pets always listen with an open heart, and it feels great to get your worries off your chest.

REST - What can you do to sleep a little more? A little better?

- Don't exercise late at night.
- Create a relaxing habit in the hour before you're going to go to bed.
- Start shutting off lights in your home an hour before you go to bed.
- Limit cell phone, computer, tv right before bed.

#3:

DO SOMETHING YOU "ALWAYS WANTED TO DO"

start something you've always wanted to do and make it part of your routine—even when it's hard to do every day. the reward often comes when the novelty wears off.

take a cooking class…get your budget under control…go skydiving…take a computer class… travel…write a book…bungee jumping…drive a semi…try your hand at painting…refinish a piece of furniture…ride a motorcycle…move & live somewhere else…arrange flowers…learn another language… reach out to a neighbor… volunteer…start a group…compose a piece of music…go to the jungle… speak up… build your "own" (shelves/garden/furniture/house/airplane/invention)...learn to play an instrument…race the Iditarod…create a website…get a new job (one you like)…go bowling…start a business… take a communication class…join a choir… join a health club…take a dance class…stretch…get a facial…start a blog… find your true joy in life...

go to a club that plays a style of live music that you don't usually listen to…go on a first date…remodel a room in your home…tell your family and friends what is REALLY important to you…change out those old floors / faucets / counters / light fixtures…do something only "crazy" people do…plant a rose bush, bulbs, a garden…sing at the top of your lungs!…get rid of clutter—simplify your surroundings and your life (start with one small area and go from there)…learn how to play a new game…

what are **you** gonna add to the list?

Hope lies in dreams, imagination, and in the courage of those who dare to make the dreams into reality.

Jonas Salk (1914-1995)

reach out, using your gifts
and passions

·   MAKE A DIFFERENCE...

live your dreams...

(and no. it
doesn't matter
how old you
are.)   really.

Hope is like the sun, which, as we journey toward it, casts the shadow of our burden behind us.

Samuel Smiles (1812-1904)

#4: FIND THE LIGHT

Go to a park and walk.

(even if it's cold.)

(or hot.)

(or windy.)

(or you really don't feel like it.)

I'm serious.

Go outside and get a little sunlight. It will increase your energy. It will get you out of the house. Look at the horizon as you're walking, not your feet.

When we get down or depressed, we tend to burrow behind closed doors and curtains.

GO OUTSIDE!!!!!

Take a child for a walk and listen to them laugh—find the light in your surroundings and in the sound of pure joy. Holly Younggren

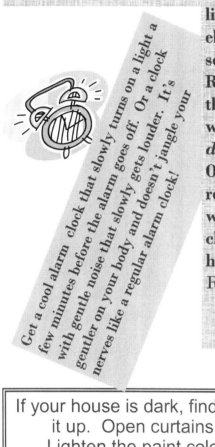

Get a cool alarm clock that slowly turns on a light a few minutes before the alarm goes off. Or a clock with gentle noise that slowly gets louder. It's gentler on your body and doesn't jangle your nerves like a regular alarm clock!

Go camping. Breaking life down to its simplest elements cleanses your soul, mind, and heart. Roasting a hotdog, throwing a ball and watching the *flames dance* in a campfire... Often, old problems reveal new solutions when you return with a clear mind and an open heart.
Ryan Younggren

If your house is dark, find ways to lighten it up. Open curtains and blinds. Lighten the paint color if it's dark.

Put brighter bulbs in at least a few light fixtures in the main areas of your house.

FINDTHELIGHT
FINDTHELIGHT
FINDTHELIGHT
FINDTHELIGHT
FINDTHELIGHT
FINDTHELIGHT
FINDTHELIGHT
FINDTHELIGHT

Make the time to...

really watch the

sunrise

sunset

Watch sunlight play upon water.
Watch a candle flame. Or flames
from a fire.

Let yourself be fascinated.

Identify things you REALLY like and surround yourself with them.

#5:

SAVOR

•

YOUR

•

FAVORITE

music • food • movies •
carpentry • sports • a
hobby • working on your
house • video games •
helping a friend •
helping a stranger •
listening to the laugh of
a young child •
teaching • parenthood •
coaching • climbing •
the season • the time of
day • landscaping •
comedians •
books • authors • fly fishing •
playing drums • reading •
bowling • dancing • talking to
friends • your favorite color •
sharing time with family •
color • painting • writing •
volunteering • watching
sports • playing them •

S
A
V
O
R

• snuggling up in your favorite
blanket on a cold, dreary day •

e n j o y play with children ·
cooking · hanging out
with your favorite
people · laughing! ·
working on your car ·
remodeling your house ·
riding motorcycles ·
shopping · make a
picture collage of your
favorite things and put
it in a very visible
place · think about what
used to give you joy
that you don't do
anymore. thank it for it's part
in your life in the past.
perhaps find a way to
incorporate that into your life
now—even if it's different.

· drinking your favorite drink on a hot
summer afternoon ·

Consciously fill your heart.

Budget time, money, & energy to do the things that are "your favorite."

#6: DO SOMETHING...

FOR SOMEONE ELSE

You know those little "How Are We Doing?" cards at the store? Take the time to fill one out when someone does an exceptional job at helping you!

Write a letter or e-mail or call a long-lost friend.

Give a stranger a compliment.

Offer your time. Volunteer.

Say a heartfelt blessing.

Smile.

Try it with the people around you—family, friends, co-workers, people you see out and about during your day. Try it when you answer the phone. Try it even when you're by yourself. See what happens to your attitude.

Send someone special a card for no reason at all.

Let a loved one know how much you really love and appreciate them.

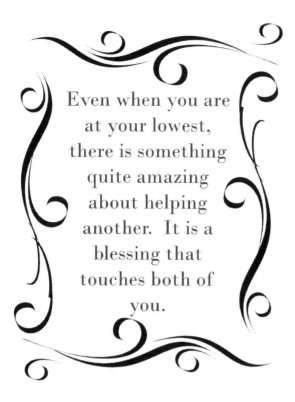

Even when you are at your lowest, there is something quite amazing about helping another. It is a blessing that touches both of you.

This is one of my personal favorite tools.

I do this when I'm "up," but especially focus on it when I'm "down." There is something powerful about helping another person. It will change your heart and your perspective. It will allow you to be more creative, and spend your energy focused on the positive. It will shift your perspective on your own stuff.

Do something special for someone anonymously. It's hard to keep the secret, but it'll make you smile inside.

Email a co-worker, sincerely thank them for the great job they do, and give an example of what they did well.

(And copy their boss on the email.)

If someone you know is having a rough time, offer to help them with some of their daily responsibilities. Take them out to lunch. Take them dinner at home. Deliver an unexpected small gift or card with a note letting them know you care...

In this life, we cannot do great things. We can only do small things with great love...
Do not wait for leaders;
do it alone, person to person.
Mother Teresa (1910-1997)

Hang out with people who you admire and want to be more like.

#7:

WHO DO YOU LOOK UP TO?

WHO'S YOUR HERO?

Role Model (rōl mŏd'l)
A person who serves as an example of the values, attitudes, and behaviors associated with a role.

****

Mentor (mĕn'tôr')
A wise and trusted counselor or teacher.

****

A **Role Model** shows you **WHAT** you want to be like.

A **Mentor** shows you **HOW** to do it.

Both can be your inspiration.

Find out how others have dealt with similar challenges that you are facing.

It's amazing how much you will learn once you begin to share and be transparent.

Say **THANK YOU.**

Looking back, recognize people who have helped you along your path—

THANK THEM! Track down your daily mentors, but also take time to thank family members, friends, co-workers, authors, speakers, teachers, medical professionals (or any professionals, for that matter) who have made an impact on your life.

Go out of your way to find people who have successfully travelled your path—they can guide you. It could be someone in your daily life whom you admire, or someone you know personally OR an author, speaker, blogger who is an expert on a subject you need guidance on.

For more ideas, see Resources on page 106.

Fill in the blank.

What would you put here?

Yes, you read that right.

#8: Plan something to look forward to

KITCHEN

BAT

DINING NOOK

Focusing on making FUTURE PLANS gets you out of worry or boredom in the present.
It gives you a sense of MOVEMENT.

Hope doesn't come from calculating whether the good news is winning out over the bad. It's simply a choice to take action.

Anna Lappé,

O Magazine

Shop and plan for a special meal.

Make a date with a family member or friend you don't see often.

Invite a friend to meet you for lunch.

Take a class. (Check your local recreation center or look into "free" universities in your area.)

Set future goals so that you have something to anticipate.

Find out what concerts or plays are coming up at the local high school or college.

Look up a favorite band and see if they are playing near you any time this year.

Buy music you used to love to listen to.

Make that appointment you have been "meaning to make..."

MARK ANNIVERSARY DATES OF "JOY" EVENTS.

THEY DON'T HAVE TO BE "BIG" TO ANYONE ELSE BUT YOU.

Get ready to Celebrate the good stuff!

Share your triumphs with others.

#9:

Do fifty sit-ups.

Walk a mile.

Smile at everyone you meet today.

Do
something
Different

Stay up all night watching a movie trilogy.

Buy a fruit or vegetable that you've never tried before.

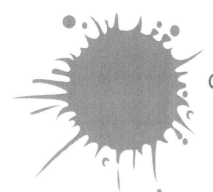

Paint a wall a different color.

LOOK AT YOUR OPTIONS — MAKE A CHOICE

Move your knickknacks and mementos from one room to another. Or, store them for a few months and pull them out later—and enjoy them again!

The first step is to fill your life with a positive faith that will help you through anything.

The second is to begin where you are.

Norman Vincent Peale (1898-1993)

Whisper when you're ANGRY.

 **DO**

Listen to uplifting music when you're feeling down.

Move your photos and paintings around.

Switch it up — hang them in different places. Whether or not you like it right off, just give it a few days.

C-H-A-N-G-E your environment

SOME

SHIFT...

YOUR

FURNITURE

AROUND

 THE

ROOM

Try tea instead of coffee

Apologize sincerely.

...To someone against whom you've been holding a grudge.

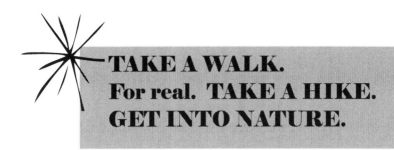

TAKE A WALK.
For real. TAKE A HIKE.
GET INTO NATURE.

Try something that you haven't tried since you were a kid.

THING

Have an actual conversation... With a living person.

Face to face. ;)

Go to an ethnic store and buy (and try) at least two food items whose ingredients you cannot read.

Different

#10:

laugh

SPEND TIME WITH HAPPY PEOPLE.

Stress-related hormones actually decrease when you laugh

#11:

Laugh

Belly laugh.

The human race only has one really effective weapon, and that is laughter.

Mark Twain (1835-1910)

It's super funny when someone snorts when they're laughing really hard, huh?

LAUGH

#12:

Once when I was having a particularly hard time, I researched laughter. I found that some people force themselves to laugh. Kind of like "fake it 'til you make it." You pretend to laugh, heeheehee hahaha hohoho, and you sound sooooo silly that you usually crack yourself up and start to laugh for real. It relieves some tension immediately. (But only do it when you're alone…or with children who get it.)

Studies show that people who laugh more and are able to look at the funnier side of life in a healthy way have healthier immune systems, improved health, increased life expectancy, and feel better overall.

Hang out for a while with a happy toddler. Their laughter is CONTAGIOUS.

Determine to live life with flair and laughter

Maya Angelou

Find a joke, picture, website, or video that ALWAYS ALWAYS makes you smile or laugh.

Use as often as necessary.

Value your friends, family, and pets that make you laugh.

Laughter increases your heart rate, exercises your facial muscles and helps you breathe more deeply.

And it gets rid of excess gas.

(Bathroom humor is almost always funny.)

Count your blessings.

#13:

g.r.a.t.i.t.u.d.e.
...is a gift

Being thankful changes your mindset. When you are agitated, frustrated, down, or feeling hopeless, make the choice to take the time to be thankful. Start with no less than ten things. If you're really, really upset, try at least twenty. It helps to shift your perspective of what's really important in your life, doesn't it?

Thank you

I have a friend who writes a "gratitude list" twice a year.

Thank you

She starts at the top of her head and writes down all the body parts she is thankful for. Her hair. Her hearing, Her voice (she is a musician.) Her eyes and her vision. She extends the list to the rest of her SELF, and moves onto gifts around her—her family, friends, home, job, health, circumstances, etc.

Thank you

Do you take these things for granted?

Thank you

What if you made a list like this?

If you lost some or all of the things on your list, would you be more thankful if you could get them back?

Send a thank you note, text, or e-mail to someone who's done you right.

Ok. Simple.

But we forget. Because we get "busy."

Gosh sakes—remember to always say

"Please" & "Thank you!"

Taking the first step

TAKING THE FIRST STEP:

The simple act of doing something different creates **HOPE**. And having renewed **HOPE** creates more change. Instead of a vicious cycle, it's creative, it builds, and it gives life <u>to</u> you instead of sapping it <u>from</u> you.

HOPE is not just a dream or a wish.

True **HOPE** is created by action. By choosing to look for the best. Focusing on the positive. Choosing gratitude as an action through which to look at your life. Each day.

> *Hope is with you in your darkness and yearns to be discovered. Part of finding hope is truly feeling your sadness, your despair. But another part is also allowing hope to pull you through and bring you into the light.*
>
> *Katharine Zink*

Even if you really work on them daily, the results from the tools in this book aren't permanent. You need to practice, and get better at using them, every day.

I know. I know. **I know.**

Life gets busy. Out of control. Chaotic. Not enough time. Not enough money. Not enough energy. LIFE HAPPENS.

You get to decide how YOU are going to react when life gets you down. Or confused. Or when it knocks you down—either because of your choices, or through no fault of your own. You need to decide whether to hang your head and look down or decide to look up and MOVE into **HOPE**.

HOPE without action or choice is hollow. **HOPE** coupled with a choice, a step, a plan, is MIGHTY. Once you really become conscious and aware of this simple truth, you will have the chance to begin to change.

> **You must be the change you wish to see in the world.**
>
> Mohandus Ghandi (1869-1948)

> **Change your thoughts and you change your world.**
>
> Norman Vincent Peale (1898-1993)

> **The strongest principle of growth lies in human choice.**
> Mary Ann Evans—
> Pen name George Eliot (1819-1880)

"It's really all about your future, the future you create every day in the small choices you make. Who are you, if not an aggregate of the choices you have made to this point in your life?

Once you grasp the connection between the choices you make and the kind of person you are becoming, you realize that there is no such thing as an insignificant choice.

They all count.

Who do you want to be?

The truth is, we get asked that question many times a day. And we answer it with our choices."

Dr. Jeffrey A. Zink, *Choices*

BIG PICTURE:
steps to making lasting change:

My mom shared a change model years ago with me. It's a great tool for understanding how change works and why it can be so hard and feel so awkward when you first start making changes.

1) Unconscious incompetence – you don't really know you're messing up. You may see the results of messing up, and hopefully you eventually get the message...but it usually takes some big "hit" in your life for you to see that there's a problem.

2) Conscious incompetence – Now you know you're messing up, but don't really know how to go about fixing it. Or you don't really want to go about fixing it. Now you're looking for excuses OR you're looking for tools and options which will help you make better choices and will ultimately help you to change.

<u>THIS is the point of choice.</u>

Make a change

OR

ignore what you just discovered.

3) Conscious competence – You've decided to take a step. You're looking for more tools to help you on your path. Support systems to help you change. A role model or mentor to help you on your way. A book with a really good philosophy or plan that makes you think and decide to take action. Steps that you start to follow. Good habits that you begin to make YOUR OWN. You may not be very good at this new thing you're trying, and despite that, it feels good to try something new. You have to think about it a lot. It's a *conscious* effort. You're moving forward, and maybe making mistakes and taking a few steps backwards, but you're <u>moving</u>!

4) Unconscious competence – Now you're doing your new habit without even really thinking about it. And you're good at it. NOW, you're the one other people are looking at saying "hey – look at them – I want to be like that."

LITTLE PICTURE DETAILS:

steps to make lasting change:

1) DECIDE / BE WILLING: The first step to changing anything is to decide to do it, to make a choice. It's simple, but it's not necessarily easy. Being willing is really the first step.

2) BABY STEPS: Next, plan a couple of small steps toward change that you can do easily and quickly.

3) SUPPORT: Confide in someone you trust. Tell them a little about your goal. Having that support and accountability will help you move, especially during times when you don't want to!

4) CUT YOURSELF SOME SLACK: Realize that change doesn't come easy. You may have an "I took one step forward and two steps back" kind of day. **HOPE** means that you commit to get back up and keep going forward REGARDLESS of the circumstances.

HOPE looks for the lesson to be learned.
HOPE looks for the chance to build:

- Yourself

  - Others

    - Relationships

      - Your legacy

What are you building right now that will go beyond you and touch people you've never even met?

Having and building **HOPE** doesn't mean you'll always be "UP". It doesn't mean you'll always be CHEERY and BRIGHT. It means that you commit to bouncing back quickly – looking for the lesson, the gift, or the wisdom to be gained from your situation.

TOOLS OF HOPE are quick and simple tools. Use them to get your head screwed back on straight. Use them to gain perspective so that you can use wisdom and discernment to make choices in making your next steps.

Using them will restore and renew your **HOPE** temporarily. Get them into your habits, and it will restore your **HOPE** regularly.

My very best to you— *ANA-CHRISTINA*

AUTHOR'S ENDNOTES:

True, down deep in your bones **HOPE:**

You know, the bottom line is that life, at its very best, can still be difficult. Busy-ness gets the best of you every day. Or maybe boredom and complacency come to visit (and they stay). You get your priorities mixed up and life starts going crooked. It doesn't look like what you thought it would.

At its worst, life can leave you feeling lonely, empty, and in pain. Reeling, confused, and desperate. Pain and futility steal your courage and instead of standing up and fighting, you curl up in despair.

I've only found one thing that ever gave me a lasting sense of hope. Through my own failures, poor choices, and wounds, through dark and troubled times, I've held onto the one truth that could reach me any time, any where, through any <u>thing.</u>

The truth, for me, has been the grace of God. He is my final, and truly, my only, Tool of Hope.

I was born in Texas and grew up in Colorado in a big, wonderful family as the oldest of five girls. My parents have a strong faith in God and we grew up in that environment. Even though I prayed growing up, I strayed once I left home and went to college in Colorado and then Wyoming. I tell some of my story in the Foreword at the beginning of the book, but here's the real deal.

Looking back, I know that my prayers along with those of my parents and aunts and grandmother are what got me through those dark, dark curl-up-in-the-corner-of-the-room moments.

Starting over is scary.

Starting over is hard.

After my escape, I was a heartbroken single mom, and my boys were confused and hurting. How to explain that staying would have been worse than leaving?

For many nights after I left, I would cry and pray. I had a favorite scripture that helped me through, and still serves as my guide:

"Praise be to the God...of all compassion and the God of all comfort, who comforts us in all our troubles, so that we can comfort those in any trouble with the comfort we ourselves have received from God." 2 Cor. 3-4 (NIV version)

I was holding on, day by healing day. I was attending twelve weeks of classes held at Gateway Battered Women's Shelter in Denver.

Slowly, I learned and grew and the pain lessened. I was finally able, truly, to help others with "the help that I myself had received." What a blessing that was!

Seven years later, I found myself at a weekend women's retreat. What I hadn't realized was that it was EXACTLY seven years, TO THE DAY AND DATE after I'd left the island and the boys' dad. It was the 7th anniversary of my arrival here in Denver. I invited Christ into my heart that weekend and it became an anniversary of change, hope and freedom rather than "escape." Only God could turn the wound into the gift.

Within the year, I'd found a church, I'd gotten my finances in order and I was out of debt, and, best of all, another "guardian angel" came to me and helped me to forgive.

I had been so angry and had become embittered toward my ex-husband. And myself. She showed me what God wanted me to see. Amazing things happen when you forgive. I know what it's like to live in bitterness and anger. It's a poison that seeps into your heart and into your soul and touches every part of your life whether you're aware of it or not.

I simply could not be the woman, mother, daughter, sister, friend, and co-worker that I wanted to be with that sickening poison in my heart.

You don't have to be perfect to ask God into your life. Asking Christ to be the Lord of your life will not make you perfect. Nor will it make your life perfect. We are human. We are flawed. We hurt others. We get hurt. We say and do stupid things that we regret later.

And He still loves us. He is the greatest **HOPE** there is.

One of my dear friends shared with me that "God expects us to participate in our recovery, and not to sit back and expect that there's no more work to be done once He enters our life. It's just that it's so much easier when He is by our side."

Maybe you had that heart-relationship with God once, and walked away. Maybe you have it and need to remind yourself of its importance. Maybe someone "religious" turned you off to God. Or maybe you want it for the first time.

As long as you're breathing, it's never too late.

If you want and long for a foundation. An anchor in the storm. A strength that is there for you no matter what is thrown at you. If you want to know that you are loved, even in your darkest night. If you want to heal your broken heart, your sickness, your confusion, He is there.

All you have to do is open up your heart and ask Him to come in. He is gentle. He won't force you. He is strong and will not leave you.

He gives strength to the weary and increases the power of the weak...But those who hope in the Lord will renew their strength . They will soar on wings like eagles; they will run and not grow weary, they will walk and not be faint. Isaiah 41:29-31 (NIV)

It's not a one-time fix. It's a yearning to continue to look up and into **HOPE** and to continue to heal and grow and share.

So.

Make a choice.

Dare to make a move.

Take a step.

Toward God. Toward the One who sacrificed so that you could have hope. Not only here, but forever. It's amazing.

Ask and it will be given to you; Seek and you will find; Knock and the door will be opened to you. For everyone who asks receives; he who seeks finds; and to him who knocks, the door will be opened. Matthew 7:7-8 (NIV)

HOW?

Go to God. In church if that's where your comfort level is. Or with a person of strong faith who will stand by you and will pray for you. Or by yourself. God is there. He sees. He hears. He knows.

Kneel and give your heart to Him. Be humble. Surrender. Say a simple prayer. It could go something like this:

> *Oh Lord – I know I'm not perfect. I am flawed and have hurt myself and others. Through that, I know I've hurt You. Please, come into my life and forgive me. You gave your Son, Jesus, so that I could be free. So that I'd have peace and life. Joy and love. A fullness in my heart that only You can give.*
>
> *I will move toward getting to know You – through the Bible, through other believers, through a church or worship service, through inspiring music, through seeing You in the world around me..*
>
> *Through gratitude and a grateful spirit. I will move toward You with an open heart. Give me a hunger for You. I know You love me unreservedly, unconditionally, and relentlessly. Thank You for opening your hands and your heart to me. Amen.*

God loves us in a lot of ways. Through people, through music, through circumstances, through nature. Open your heart to look for it, to listen, and to feel.

WHAT THEN?

Time to make some more changes! Take little steps. Read the Bible (the Psalms have really good prayers.) Check out some churches. Check out Christian music. Write your thoughts and prayers to God in a journal.

And the rest of the story...

In my life, God has been really big on changing that "escape anniversary" into other anniversaries. I've changed my career: I had worked through Dan Miller's *48 Days to the Work You Love Workbook* and it made me realize that my life was very much out of balance. I worked on balancing my life, centering my heart, learning new skills.

Miracles have happened. My heart has swelled and grown and forgiveness and healing of old wounds has led to a most amazing life—one I never could have imagined.

Regardless of your life circumstances, regardless of your financial situation, or your family of origin, or your current family dynamic or your health issues, God offers you peace. What He helps you to do is to have the stability that comes from having your life anchored in Him.

What that anchor brings is strength to pursue life. To choose how to approach it.

Daily.

With a willing heart

With strength

With purpose

With vulnerability

With passion

With humor

With compassion

With humility

With courage, confidence, gentleness, kindness

With love, healing, growth, generosity

With **HOPE**

I've used the tools in my book. They helped me get through some of my roughest times.

I breathe quite regularly. (ha!) Sometimes, it's the only thing that gets me through certain moments.

Something Different? I have taken glass fusion classes, glass-blowing classes, I have bungee jumped, I have remodeled my home, I decided to learn how to grow orchids because all other plant matter soon meets its demise in my house, and now have over 25 plants in a huge tank by my front window...I published two books and a set of prayer cards...I learned how to ride a motorcycle and it's a fire-engine red sport bike—& take myself to the mountains all the time to sit by moving water (one of my passions.) I've learned to open my heart and be willing to love again.

And yes, I've had some moments in the last few years where I asked myself, "Hey, what'd you write in the book, anyway? Why don't you do it?" And I usually do.

My desire for you is that you will make some choices and act on them. To follow through with small steps. To make changes and create habits that stay with you for the rest of your days. That you would make a difference during your time here, and not take it for granted. That you would support others and help them along the path that you've already taken – because you've gone further than they have, and you can guide them and make their journey a little easier.

That you would have **HOPE** and carry it with you in your heart.

ANA-CHRISTINA

www.toolsofhope.com   hope@toolsofhope.com

My friend Beth, sent me this poem shortly after I landed in Colorado. I lost track of her soon after—I do not know if she wrote it or if the author is unknown. It gave me tremendous hope and strength during hard times.

ANOTHER DAY

Another day has taught me
the steady trot will still.

Another day has brought me
some time bought with will.

Another week will teach me "I AM", a warrior's cry.
Another week will buy me the time alone to try.

Another month will test me
on memories much too dear.

Another month will lease me
the strength to conquer fear.

Another year will teach me to sing a lullaby.

Another year will buy me the wings to fly the sky.

Another life has taught me the blessing of "I CAN".

**Another life has bought me
respect and thoughts that stand.**

To my dear friend
so that the days
will not callous you.
- Author Unknown

Resources:

Websites and authors that have provided me and mine with real-life tools that help:

Life & Career Skills:

48Days.com / *48 Days to the Work You Love*—Dan Miller / *No More Mondays*—Dan Miller

- *Choices—Using Values to Make Good Choices Every Day*— Dr. Jeffrey A. Zink

Money Stuff:

- TotalMoneyMakeover.com / *More Than Enough*—Dave Ramsey / *The Total Money Makeover— A Proven Plan for Financial Success*—Dave Ramsey (books and cd's) (p.s. Dave's use of humor has kept me in my car, listening to him, long after I reached my destination. He is an awesome speaker and presenter.)

Parenting:

- LoveAndLogic.com / *Parenting with Love and Logic*— Foster W. Cline and Jim Fay (Huge array of books and cd's along with free articles at their website.) (These cd's are soooo funny—you'll laugh at the stories while you're learning!)

Domestic Violence:

- DomesticViolence.org / Even though this is a Michigan-based website, it has great general information on what D.V. is, common myths, the violence wheel, the cycle of violence, why women stay, how to get out, and other resources

- 24 hour hotline, all 50 states / 1-800-799-7233 / National Domestic Violence Hotline / NDVH.org

Communication

- The Confident Communicator—
www.toolsofhope.com—Ana-Christina
- CBPG—Communicating by Personality Group—
www.toolsofhope.com—Ana-Christina

Relationships:

- ColorCode.com / *The Color Code—A New Way to See Yourself, Your Relationships, and Life*—Dr. Taylor Hartmann

- *The Five Love Languages—How to Express Heartfelt Commitment to Your Mate*—Gary Chapman (book or cd)

- *Love & Respect: The Love She Most Desires; The Respect He Desperately Needs*—Emerson Eggrichs

- *Date or Soul Mate: How to Know if Someone is Worth Pursuing in Two Dates or Less*—Dr. Neil Clark Warren / *Finding the Love of Your Life*—Dr. Neil Clark Warren

- *Mars and Venus on a Date: A Guide for Navigating the Five Stages of Dating to Create a Loving and Lasting Relationship*—John Gray

- *Laugh your Way to a Better Marriage*—Mark Gungor

  Super, super funny and informative.

- *Boundaries*—Dr. Henry Cloud & Dr. John Townsend

- *How Al-Anon Works for Families and Friends of Alcoholics*—Al-Anon Family Group Head Inc.

Uplifting Music:

- *Positive and encouraging music— WWW.KLOVE.COM—find a local radio station.*

Author's Acknowledgement:

Thank you. Thank you most of all to my Lord, Christ Jesus. For the strength, the courage, the blessing, and my growth.

Glory to Him, who, working through us, can do infinitely more than we can ask or imagine. Ephesians 3:20.

I want to thank my children, Colin, Nicholas, and Christopher. Big hug and biggest love.

I thank my family—You have been and continue to be, my giants. Mom & Dad—I hold you in the highest esteem. You've created and built a wonderful family. I admire your generosity, your nurturing, your strength. Mamane Julieta—the strong matriarch without whom we wouldn't be here...And the "Varela girls", my sisters: Alissa, Tania, Laura, and Teressa. You have always been there for me—concerned and lifting me up in the hard times. Celebrating and whooping it up for the good times. To the Rosario, Navarrete, Varela families. Thank you for the prayers and concern, the conversation, the healing, and the huge, hurt-my -belly, run-out-of-breath laughs. Thank you for everything. I love you.

To all of the hearts who have helped me and my boys along the path. For your support, help, faith, prayer, and laughs. To Naomi and Chikayo who got us to the airport safely. To Mike Dahl, who got us to our next flight.

To Carol—who got me out. To Rocio—who got me up.

To Vickie who received the very first "copy" of this book written on index cards in the top of a toolbox for her new apartment and her new life.

To my editing team—Holly, Ryan, Julie W., Jeffrey, Katharine, Mike Dee. You poked and questioned and polished and MADE IT BETTER. Your comments were priceless.

To my special team, dance-in-the-room-go-for-it final technical editor, Rose. You all rock.

Jeffrey—You encouraged me when I needed it. You prodded me when I didn't want to go there. You tempered me when I just wanted to blow and go. And you fired me up when I needed more steam. Thanks for believing in this project.

Katharine—your insight is unbelievable. You're wonderful.

2014 edition: Life has brought unbelievable change since this book was first published. Pain, joy, triumph, sorrow. Growth. Above everything, growth. And learning. !!

How you choose to frame up the events that happen to you makes all the difference. I choose to learn and be grateful despite the circumstances, in spite of the confusion and uncertainty.

Even if, even though, even when...

Special thanks to Susan Berry, Jim Darr, Alicia Ames, Lucille Dupuis, and Wilson Hicks. Wilson—you went from co-worker to friend to gift to my husband and bond. I love you so. You have taught me what faith looks like, you've taught me to open my heart, to love more, to laugh more, and to live more.

Faith has to do with things that are unseen and Hope with things that are not at hand.

St. Thomas Aquinas (1225-1274)

Made in USA - Crawfordsville, IN
66208_9781086428506
10.25.2021 1121